19 February – 19 March

amber
BOOKS

ASTROLOGICAL SIGN DATES:
The precise start and end times for each sign vary by a day or two from year to year as the Gregorian calendar shifts relative to the tropical year. The dates provided in this book are correct for the year 2020.

If you are unsure of the Zodiac sign for your specific birth year, visit: www.yourzodiacsign.com.

19 February – 19 March

A guide to understanding yourself, your friendships and finding your true love

This edition first published in 2020 by
Amber Books Ltd
United House
North Road
London N7 9DP
United Kingdom
www.amberbooks.co.uk
Instagram: amberbooksltd
Facebook: amberbooks
Twitter: @amberbooks

ISBN: 978-1-83886-033-2

Project Editor: Sarah Uttridge
Design: Zoë Mellors

Picture Credits:
All illustrations by Fabbri Publications except the following:
Shutterstock: 32 (Elena Naumchenkova), 33 (La Puma), 36 (Slonomysh), 41 (Angel Soler Gollonet)

Printed and bound in China

TRADITIONAL CHINESE BOOKBINDING

This book has been produced using traditional Chinese bookbinding techniques, using a method that was developed during the Ming Dynasty (1368–1644) and remained in use until the adoption of Western binding techniques in the early 1900s. In traditional Chinese binding, single sheets of paper are printed on one side only, and each sheet is folded in half, with the printed pages on the outside. The book block is then sandwiched between two boards and sewn together through punched holes close to the cut edges of the folded sheets.

Contents

Introduction

Pisces

19 February–19 March

Sign: Two Fish
Ruling Planet: Neptune and Jupiter
Gender: Feminine
Element: Water
Quality: Mutable

Compatibility: Aquarius, Pisces and Virgo
Non-compatibility: Cancer, Scorpio and Capricorn

Every man, woman and child is born with a distinct and different destiny. There are no exceptions. Everyone has cosmic significance and a part to play in the life of the universe. This is innate and inescapable, and goes beyond the tiny boundaries of nation, creed and colour.

As we live out our lives on planet Earth, we are, however unknowingly, acting in a greater drama and reacting to impulses that come from distant astronomical bodies, stars and planets millions of light years away. Sceptics pour scorn on the idea that far-distant Saturn, for example, can have any effect on our lives, as the ancient art and science of astrology teaches. But the fact is that we are sparks of energy inhabiting bodies made of the same stuff as the stars, responding like tiny radios to the distant messages they send to Earth.

Each infant carries within it a double blueprint for life: its genetic programming and the pattern of character that comes from the astrological 'clock' that was set in motion at the moment of birth. No one knows the full extent of genetic influence, although it seems to be astonishingly far-reaching, but the power of the horoscope has been well known to the wisest men and women for many centuries.

Our Sun and Moon signs provide essential inside information about our destinies. They reveal the secrets of who we really are, and why we are here, laying out before us our potential, the sort of joys and achievements our characteristics may bring about, and warn us of problems to be overcome through the triumph of free will.

Read this book with an open mind and discover who you really are.

The Elements

Up to the beginning of the Age of Enlightenment – the modern scientific era – in the 18th century, it was commonly believed that everything, including human beings, was made up of the four elements: Earth, Air, Fire and Water. These were thought of as the building blocks of life, and each astrological sign had a predominance of one or another. Each created its common characteristics, although too much of any of the elements can produce an unbalanced personality.

Water Signs

The Water signs are Cancer, Scorpio and Pisces. They are emotional, intuitive and often psychic, strongly in touch with the hidden, mysterious side of life and with the ebb and flow of unseen energies. Like the ocean tides, they have surges of inspiration and bursts of euphoria, or they can be plunged into gloom and introspection. Cancerians are emotionally tied to their homes and families; just like their sign, the Crab, they jealously guard their own particular little rock pool, hiding their softest feelings under a hard shell.

Scorpians are the occultists and profound thinkers of the zodiac, very sexy and magnetic, but sometimes too intense. They are the still waters that run deep – very, very deep.

Pisceans' emotions can lie undisturbed for long periods, then suddenly rise to the surface. They can be fast and elusive – slippery customers sometimes – and change direction for no apparent reason, often against their own best interests. But, like the other two Water signs, they operate almost entirely through their feelings, which can be very positive when set against the dour practicality of a Capricornian or the most reliable investment banker of a Taurean. They can give some depth to the adventures of the Arian and the madcap schemes of the Geminian, and reveal some of the mysteries of the Universe, which is never a bad thing.

Water Signs
Cancer
Scorpio
Pisces

Colours of the Zodiac

Traditionally, each sign of the zodiac has its own colour, which is believed to be 'lucky' or magically empowered for those born under that particular sign. In general, the colours are associated with the ruling planets and are symbolic of their attributes. Many people find that they feel most comfortable when wearing their sign's colours, and often choose them without knowing their full astrological background.

Pisces

Ruling Planet: Neptune.

Colours: Sea green and mauve.

Evocative of the ocean, seaweed and myths about mermaids, these greens encourage the ebb and flow of emotion, but should be worn sparingly. Pisceans need to get their feet on the ground occasionally.

The Angelic Hierarchy

According to ancient tradition, each planet is governed by one of the great archangels, who are also rulers of certain aspects of human life. The box below lists the planet that they rule, the areas over which they have influence and their special day of the week.

Asariel

Archangel of Neptune.

Governs: Pisces.

Rules: The waters of the earth; the seas, oceans and the rivers.

Day: Asariel is not associated with a particular day.

The Genders

Traditionally, the twelve signs of the zodiac are divided into Masculine and Feminine, although of course both men and women are born into each.

The characteristics were assigned to the genders aeons ago, well before modern feminism or political correctness, and may now seem old-fashioned to many. However, the signs do seem to be grouped according to the appropriate gender.

The Feminine Signs

The Feminine signs are Taurus, Cancer, Virgo, Scorpio, Capricorn and Pisces. Feminine traits tend to be most accentuated in the Water signs of Cancer and Pisces.

These signs present gentler, more passive qualities. They are the carers and the nurturers, inclined to take a back seat and worry over the well-being of others. They are artistic and in tune with their intuition, and may be psychic. Self-evidently, these are the motherly and sisterly signs, with all the attendant positive and negative characteristics. They tend to be the power behind the throne, rather than movers and shakers, although many are great achievers, especially in the modern, more egalitarian world, where their qualities are encouraged.

Negatively, the Feminine signs can be fussy, possessive, mean-minded, vindictive, cringing, clinging and over-emotional.

Aquarius, the sign of the coming Age, is endowed with both Masculine and Feminine traits, although it is traditionally categorized as Masculine.

The Ruling Planets

Until the 18th century, astrologers knew only the planets of our solar system that could be seen with the naked eye: Mercury, Venus, Mars, Jupiter and Saturn. (For the purposes of astrology, the Sun and the Moon are also counted as planets even though the Sun is a star and the Moon is the satellite of Earth.) Uranus was discovered in 1781, Neptune in 1846 and Pluto was first seen in 1930. Many astrologers believe that the existence of other heavenly bodies – such as the rumoured Vulcan, which hypothetically exists within the orbit of Mercury – is about to be confirmed. Astrologers will then have to agree which signs these 'new' planets will rule, and what human characteristics their discovery will accentuate.

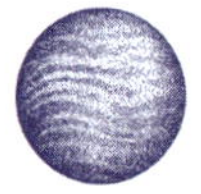

Neptune

Neptune was the Roman version of the Greek god of the sea, Poseidon. He was often depicted as a bearded man rising from the depths clutching a trident, the symbol of his power.

About Neptune

Neptune was discovered in 1846 and is approximately 45,000 million km (28,000 million miles) away from the Sun, which it takes 165 years to orbit.
Neptune has two moons.
Neptune has no sacred day but, by association with the Moon, which rules the sea, Monday may be considered a suitable candidate.

Astrologically, Neptune is associated with artistic expression, especially dancing and poetry – and also with illusion. The planet can encourage fine creativity, but at the same time mislead the unwary into the dead end of illusory activities such as gambling or obsessive daydreaming. Pisces is ruled by Neptune. Pisceans, the dreamy, artistic, indecisive and sometimes even deceitful sign, reflect Neptune's curious power. There is an element of insubstantial promises about Neptune, like wishes in fairy stories. They may come true, to the letter, but in a cruelly deceptive way.

Jupiter

Jupiter was the Greco-Roman god of plenty, also known as Jove or, in ancient Greece, Zeus. He was the protecting father-god of the city of Rome.

Traditionally deemed a 'lucky' planet by astrologers, Jupiter is the ruler of Sagittarius and

About Jupiter

A far-distant 778 million km (484 million miles) from the Sun, the planet Jupiter measures a massive 145,000 km (90,000 million miles) across. It is the largest heavenly body in our solar system, although much of its mass is composed of hydrogen and helium.

Jupiter's sacred day is Thursday.

Pisces, although Pisces is now ruled by Neptune, and is associated with joy, plenty, philosophy and all manner of academic study.

The Qualities

In addition to the influence of gender, the elements and the planets, each sign of the zodiac is affected by having an intrinsic quality – Cardinal, Fixed or Mutable.

Mutable Quality

Those born under the Mutable signs are always on the move, either physically or mentally, forever seeking fresh fields and pastures new. They are restless, versatile and flexible, hating routine and any form of strict discipline. These individuals can have butterfly minds, endlessly alighting on new enthusiasms, fads or crazes, then dropping them just as quickly and moving on to the next thing. Mutable people can be unreliable and irresponsible, and are rarely self-disciplined, although they are often extremely charming.

Pisces

Emotional, insecure Pisceans are creative and intuitive, but can often seem adrift in the everyday world. They seek peace, harmony and love, and can tend to have a somewhat unrealistic view of life. In some cases, this is all that gets them through, because a negative side of this sign is the ease with which Pisceans lose incentive and take refuge in escapism and illusion.

Signs and Symbols

Most people are familiar with the zodiac 'zoo' – the collection of symbols that represent the twelve signs. These images reflect the characteristics traditionally assigned to each sign and contain a wealth of knowledge about its true nature.

Each sign of the zodiac is represented by a symbol – the twin fish for Pisces, for example. No one is sure exactly when or why the symbols were chosen, although some authorities believe they date from Sumeria or Mesopotamia, 4000 years before Jesus Christ. The priest-astrologers of the ancient world were the first to impose recognizable patterns on the great constellations – Leo the Lion being one example.

Today, seeing such shapes in the stars may seem fanciful, but thousands of years ago imaginations were more poetic, and many myths told of magical animals, such as the dragon, which had strange powers to influence everyday human life.

Although the ancient Egyptians left few astrological records, they were almost unique in antiquity for worshipping archetypal, animal-headed gods. However, these strange hybrid gods – half-human, half-animal – were worshipped as aspects of one God. Contrary to the general belief that the Egyptians were idolaters, their religion was basically monotheistic. Each statue represented an aspect of the one true God.

Since they were established, the signs have remained unchanged, although there was a movement in the Middle Ages to change the sign of Aquarius to the sign of John the Baptist – presumably because of the connection with water.

The twelve signs of the zodiac do seem particularly apt on the whole, and accurately reflect the archetypal character of Sun sign types. The great Swiss psychoanalyst Carl Gustav Jung (1875–1961) believed that, deep in our psyches, humanity shares a collective unconscious – a set of archetypal images, which, at a profound level, we all understand. The signs of the zodiac form part of this pool of images, conveying eternal truths to our unconscious minds.

Signs and Symbols

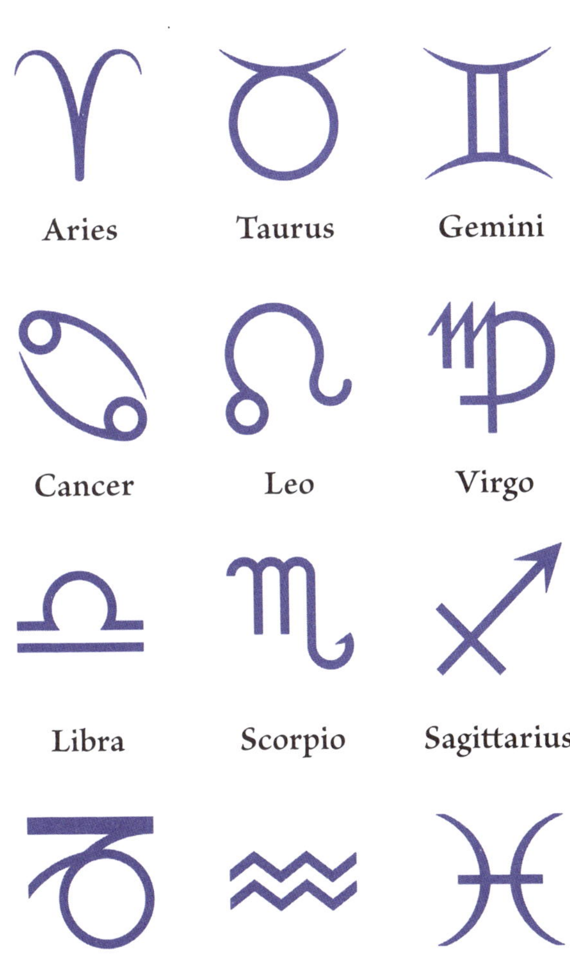

Pisces
The Fish

The symbol is two fish, sometimes apparently tied together, constantly swimming against each other and wasting their energies. Even if they are free, one fish is set to go one way while the other forever journeys in the opposite direction. This can be an apt symbol for this often contrary, dual Water sign.

Fish are notoriously difficult to catch – otherwise there would be no sport in fishing. They symbolize

the elusive and unpredictable characteristics of those sometimes slippery customers who are born under the sign of Pisces.

However, fish also go deep, sometimes to the very bottom, plumbing the depths. In dreams, water always symbolizes the hidden emotions and darkest secrets of the unconscious mind, with which many Pisceans are intuitively in touch.

The fish was an early symbol of Jesus: 'fish' in Greek was made up of the same letters as his name. In the first days of Christian persecution under the Roman Empire, the sign of the fish, scrawled on walls and doors, told fellow believers in which houses they could safely take shelter.

Many of Jesus's male disciples were originally fishermen: Simon Peter, the founder of the Christian Church and the first Pope, was affectionately known as 'the Big Fisherman' because of his unusual height. Like many of the dying-and-rising gods of his day, Jesus was known as 'the Fisher of men'. However, few today realize that this was a title that, according to the many gospels not included in the New Testament, was originally given to his close companion, Mary Magdalene, by Jesus himself.

The Sun in Pisces

Sun sign Pisceans are emotional, dreamy, insecure people with strong creative instincts. Poetic and intuitive, they often seem out of place in the everyday world. All the same, many Pisceans achieve great things. They are kind, sensitive souls, who delight in the happiness and fulfilment of others. Sometimes they go too far in this regard, for

Personality Traits of Pisceans

Positive	*Negative*
Poetic	Dreamy
Intuitive	Insecure
Kind	Indecisive
Creative	Deceitful
Compassionate	Secretive
Gentle	Emotional
Likeable	

they can live their entire lives in the shadow of other, more ambitious people, and never achieve their own true potential. Born under an archetypically Feminine Water sign, Pisceans seek above all to establish peace, harmony and love and can become terribly distressed if they fail to do so, or when others do not share their idealistic visions.

Pisceans tend to view life through rose-tinted spectacles. In some cases, this is all that gets them through, because a negative side of this sign is the ease with which Pisceans can be cast down and depressed. Once this happens, all motivation is gone and Pisceans become moody, subservient and weak-willed. Many will do anything rather than face cold, stark reality, finding refuge in escapism of one sort or another. One of their rulers, Neptune, governs illusion, and although this can manifest itself in very healthy, creative ways (see Career), it may cover some forms of addiction.

Like their sign – two fish swimming in opposite directions – Pisceans have a markedly indecisive streak. They may be afraid of offering their own opinions, although at the same time they resent it when others take command. This leads to all manner of internal tensions, sometimes erupting in crankiness. Pisceans watch more open, decisive people state their case and even if they disagree, they don't say so. Then, as time passes, they realize what they should have said, and how much difference it would have made. However, they interpret this as the fault of others, and inwardly seethe with resentment.

Pisceans are secretive, and can be deceitful. They may lack the depth and scope of black Scorpionic vengeance, but they can still be quite nasty. Of course, many are delightful, open people – after all, the full picture of any one character can only be seen accurately when the whole chart is studied – but there is almost always an underlying feeling of not belonging, of lacking a voice, and of being faceless, which manifests as resentment at the assertiveness of other people.

Appearance

Pisceans tend to be of small to medium height, and quite slightly built, although they can pack on the pounds later in life if they are not careful. They often have strangely rebellious hair and spend time and money on taming it. Pisceans have delicate eyes and, if they are pale-skinned, they often need glasses. Typically, Pisceans are strong-featured, with generous mouths and a quirky, slightly twitchy smile. It is as if they are undecided whether or not to join in the fun.

Pisceans are often very chic and take an interest in stylish clothes. Both sexes are usually well-groomed and pay attention to detail. They are rarely eccentric or look out of place, and are uncomfortable with those who do. Female Pisceans often make their own clothes, favouring luxury fabrics such as silk, velvet and satin.

Health

Pisceans are highly strung, reacting badly to all manner of pollutants, whether physical ones such as dust, smog or chemicals or emotional triggers such as rows or anxiety. Even psychic 'vibes' disturb them. These things can provoke allergies,

crippling headaches and a host of other ailments. To counter these adverse effects, Pisceans should seek protection – either through meditation or prayer or by strengthening themselves through physical exercise. Although not always naturally sporty, they should at least try to walk briskly for half an hour a day, and/or swim three times a week. However, yoga is the perfect exercise: it stretches and works the muscles while at the same time calming and invigorating the soul. Traditionally, Pisceans have trouble with their feet, and if this is a problem they should visit their chiropodist regularly, and invest as much as they can afford in good, supportive shoes.

Those born under the sign of the Fishes tend to develop addictions, and should be very wary of smoking and drinking. Pisceans sometimes tend to be hypochondriacs, reaching for the medicine cabinet at the slightest twinge, while others – an increasing number – seek out various holistic therapies. Certainly, they will fare well, on the whole, with acupressure, Chinese medicine and Reiki. However, Pisceans need to realize that many, though not all, of their health problems are psychosomatic, and result from their internalized emotions. They need to find an outlet for them.

Career

Pisceans are in touch with their unconscious minds, and once they learn to deal with this effectively, they can become successful artists. There are many top Piscean painters and poets who obey their inner voice. Many actors who may be shy and retiring off stage positively shine once hidden behind the mask of a scripted character.

However, Pisceans are dreamy people and feel threatened by too much structure, which is why the caring professions are excellent outlets for the often repressed Piscean emotion. They make superb nurses, counsellors and therapists, finding an elusive assertiveness in speaking up for the disadvantaged and physically or mentally handicapped. However, they are not natural organizers or administrators. Often, they do not seek promotion, but are more content to take a back seat and get on with their job. They are very good team members, and can rise to occasions such as major emergencies – as long as someone else is there to tell them, clearly and decisively, what to do.

Because of their tendency to various forms of addiction themselves, Pisceans are especially good with the rehabilitation of addicts, finding the right mix of compassion and tough love for the programme to succeed.

Many Pisceans find fulfilment in holistic therapies and become qualified in 'alternative' disciplines, from acupuncture to hands-on healing. They are particularly attracted to crystal therapy and rebirthing, and make natural dream analysts.

Piscean caring extends to the animal kingdom: many Pisceans are veterinary nurses or helpers in

The best careers for Pisceans

- Poet
- Nurse
- Counsellor
- Therapist
- Veterinary nurse
- Photographer
- Filmmaker
- Animator

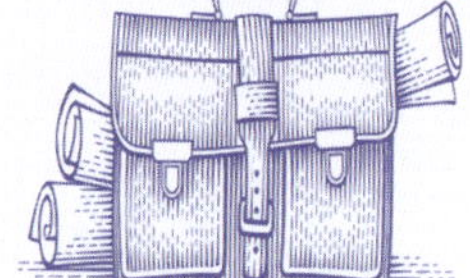

animal rescue centres. Many have a special empathy with distressed pets, and a sure instinct about how to treat their ailments, often using unorthodox methods such as homeopathy. Pisceans have plenty of imagination but not too much initiative. They hate the boisterousness of courses designed to encourage team bonding and decision-making, but may benefit from them more than most. The glamour professions also attract typical Sun sign Pisceans, who can be both artistic and moody. They are often found as dress designers, make-up artists and sometimes models. Since Neptune, their ruler, emphasizes illusion, Pisceans make good photographers, and can often be found as set designers for the theatre, television or films. They love creating a world in which others can lose themselves. Some Pisceans are cartoonists and animators, while others invent virtual worlds through computer special effects.

Pisces is one of the dual signs, and Piscean restlessness is often assuaged by having more than one job, or by pursuing a career during the day, while enjoying charity work in the evenings and at weekends. Pisceans need to keep busy, or they can easily fall prey to self-doubt and depression, and become very irritable.

Relationships

Many Pisceans can be very loving and warm partners for life, although they are too restless to settle without the occasional change of scene. They can be quite flighty, seeking to find self-esteem in the arms of many lovers, but all too often failing to do so, even though they long to be loved.

They tend to be easily bored. It is then that they find temptation of one sort or another difficult to resist, or fly into perverse, contrary moods when they become irritated with themselves and the world around them. As a result, they may hit out at their nearest and dearest, often with a deadly accuracy, instinctively knowing how best to hurt those they know well. Pisceans can usually recognize the weaknesses of others, and, if cornered, can go for them vindictively. They also do a very effective line in huge emotional scenes, although these tend to be over almost as soon as they have begun. However, the memory will continue to haunt non-Piscean witnesses for some time.

Even so, many Pisceans are truly charming, hospitable folk, who love sharing their beautiful homes with guests, family members and a menagerie

of pets. They are justly proud of their home-making skills and shine primarily as gardeners, using great imagination and artistry in the landscaping and composition of their land. Pisceans need to get out into the open air, and often love to be near to the sea. Many of them are happiest when they are living in seaside towns.

Romantic and tender-hearted, Pisceans can easily fall for rogues. Because charm works wonders with them, they are particularly vulnerable to confidence tricksters. If a day of reckoning comes and the flaws of their loved ones are revealed, it is more than usually traumatic for a typical Sun sign Piscean. They hate having their rose-tinted spectacles ripped off so cruelly, and can react by hitting out at those who dare to do so, before finally accepting the truth. Some, though, never do. Occasionally, Pisceans prefer to live with a lie rather than face facts.

Pisceans are not always the best of parents, because they are vague and self-absorbed and need to live their own lives.

Of course, many of the more well-balanced Pisceans make excellent parents, creating a loving, stable environment for their family.

Ideal Partner

Aquarians tend to bond romantically with Pisces, although they will not easily endure too many emotional outbursts or any vindictiveness. However, the organizational abilities of Aquarians often complement Piscean dreaminess very well, resulting in a beautiful home and a spiritually aware atmosphere. Two Pisceans together will never get anything done, although their dreams may be truly exciting. However, emotions will run too high with watery Cancerians. A match with a typical Sun sign Scorpian is out, though. The nastiness that can arise if things go wrong will be unbearable. However, kind, earthy Virgoans can often find happiness with Pisceans. In some cases, lordly Leos will magnanimously allow Pisceans to live in their shadow, which may well suit both of them.

Compatibility in Relationships

Aries

20 March–19 April

Domineering and inflexible Arians find oddball and effusive Pisceans too difficult to live with.

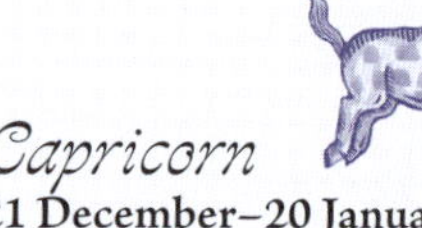

Capricorn

21 December–20 January

Four-square, unemotional Goats find Piscean excesses beyond belief, and won't even begin to woo them.

Cancer

21 June–21 July

At worst, weepy, over-the-top Cancerians and moody Pisceans make for a nightmare domestic scenario.

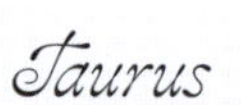

Taurus

20 April–20 May

Pisceans' innate moodiness and contrariness can seriously annoy equable, well-grounded Taureans.

Libra

23 September–22 October

The last thing peace-seeking Librans need is Piscean 'baggage' and moodiness. This relationship won't last.

Leo

22 July–22 August

Lordly Leos are very sexy and charming, but touchy Pisceans will soon back away from all that ambition.

Scorpio

23 October–21 November

While these two signs can easily fall for each other, they are far too difficult to make the necessary compromises.

Virgo

23 August–22 September

Pisceans can easily come to love Virgoans' charm and sense of order. This can be a lasting romance.

Aquarius

21 January–18 February

These two signs are soulmates and made for each other. Aquarian loftiness can easily overlook Piscean angst.

Sagittarius

22 November–20 December

Demanding Pisceans will be hurt and puzzled by the Sagittarian tendency to disappear without a word.

Gemini

21 May–20 June

There may be a strong initial attraction between these two signs, but party animal Geminians can seem too light.

Pisces

19 February–19 March

A winning combination – the organizational skills of one complementing those of the other.

The Piscean Child

The Piscean tendency to dreaming and absent-mindedness can get many children into trouble at school and also later in life. Parents should therefore encourage them to focus and concentrate as much as possible.

Often Piscean children live in their own fantasy world, and can slip all too easily into embroidering the truth. Some may be truly deceitful. The ground rules should be very clear-cut: everyone here speaks the truth. These children need to understand that being straightforward is by far the best way, and that lying is an unattractive social vice. On the other hand, it is a good idea to channel their undoubted creativity into something more acceptable, such as painting or short-story writing, in which they are often near the top of their class. All the same, they need to be taught how to separate fantasy from reality, and any tales they spin need to be taken with a pinch of salt.

It is important to establish trust between parents and Piscean children at an early age, so that there is always an atmosphere of loving support at home. These children need to feel that home is a haven, and that they have a valuable role to play there. This is vital for the development of their self-esteem, and for their future adult relationships. When they are very small, they do need strong parenting, and the knowledge that they are protected against harsh reality. These are very sensitive, sometimes weak, children, who can react badly if mishandled at an early age.

Piscean children are not good as competitors, and may easily be overpowered by their siblings. They rarely fight for what they want, usually giving in submissively. They come to idolize a more glamorous or successful brother or sister. Parents should make it clear that they have just as much to offer, in their own way, and should always praise them for their achievements and encourage their siblings to do the same.

Famous Pisceans

Michael Caine

Mikhail Gorbachev

Jean Harlow

Samuel Pepys

Glenn Miller

Alexander Graham Bell

Enrico Caruso

Buffalo Bill Cody

Albert Einstein

Bobby Fischer

Yuri Gagarin

Galilei Galileo

Michelangelo

Liza Minnelli

Rupert Murdoch

Rudolf Nuryev

Vaslav Nijinsky

Pierre-Auguste Renoir

Bugsy Siegel

Elizabeth Taylor

Finding Your Sun Sign (2020 dates)

Aries	20 March–19 April*
Taurus	20 April–20 May
Gemini	21 May–20 June
Cancer	21 June–21 July
Leo	22 July–22 August
Virgo	23 August–22 September
Libra	23 September–22 October
Scorpio	23 October–21 November
Sagittarius	22 November–20 December
Capricorn	21 December–20 January
Aquarius	21 January–18 February
Pisces	19 February–19 March

*The dates provided in this book reflect the year 2020.
Dates may vary by a day or two from year to year.